Followers of the daily broad talking about the new devotional-style book, *Straight Talk for the Journey.*

Straight Talk for the Journey is straight-up truth! Packed with wisdom, these daily devotional readings are powerful and practical words to live by. Robert Day targets our culture, our behavior, and even our hearts with surefire aim in a way that will challenge you at least, and change you for the better.
Darlene Shirley, Louisville KY

I enjoy waking up and hearing Straight Talk with Robert Day on the radio and reading his daily Facebook posts! Every believer needs encouragement and words of wisdom from time to time. Mr. Day has a powerful testimony since childhood and knows how to relate to adults and children that are enduring difficult times. He has many helpful suggestions for living life, and making positive changes in yourself and in your community.
Mercy Clements, Lynchburg VA

Robert Day is gifted with the ability to see today's world and its problems and hear answers that are clearly from God that cut right to the heart of the matter and bring relevant solutions. It is exciting to see these answers and teachings in print where they can be referred to and reflected upon by many people.
Marsha Young, Wildwood FL

We love the family friendly messages Straight Talk offers to our us every day. Our kids enjoy listening before school and it provides us with the opportunity to be inspired and talk about many social situations.
Bambi Durham, Bedford VA

Straight Talk is an encouraging reminder of God's Grace, and how we as His redeemed people can extend that Grace to others in need of healing.
Joann Payne, Portland OR

Common sense solutions for a time in which the moral fiber of our nation is on a rocky path. Take Away: Straight Talk for the Journey will refresh and nourish your soul.
Bonnie Burley Crews, Rustburg, VA

Straight Talk
WITH ROBERT DAY

Straight Talk
for the journey.

Inspirational excerpts from the
daily radio broadcast,
Straight Talk with Robert Day

ROBERT J. DAY, MSW, M.Div
CEO of Patrick Henry Family Services

Published by
Patrick Henry Family Services Publishing
1621 Enterprise Drive
Lynchburg, VA 24502
434-239-6891
patrickhenry.org

Cover design by Beckie Nix
Interior design by Jon Marken, Lamp-Post Publicity
Editing by Donna Guthrie
Marketing by Beckie Nix

Printed in the United States of America

ISBN: 978-0-9979026-3-1

A thought is as real as a cannonball.
Joubert

 # Contents

Preface

ROBERT DAY BEGAN his leadership of Patrick Henry Family Services in 2010. At that time, the nonprofit charity consisted of a handful of residential group homes for children and youth, and one counseling center. Though tenured in child welfare for more than 50 years, the ministry was limited in its capacity, and could do little more than be a place of refuge for kids who had nowhere to go.

For more than a half century Patrick Henry Boys & Girls Homes received children as young as age six, after they had been abused, neglected, and rejected. It is heartbreaking to see these precious children who had experienced so much abuse and neglect at such a young age. We could never build enough group homes to meet the needs. Part of the answer has to come through intervention of families at greatest risk, and the education of a culture spinning out of control.

This fundamental shift of change began with a renewed interest in not only being a place of refuge for vulnerable children, but also being an outreach to struggling families and fractured homes at the point of crisis, and even before the crisis occurs.

As CEO, Robert Day has remained focused on maxing out the mission of PHFS. Today the ministry also includes a home for unwed mothers and their babies, six counseling centers, a camp, retreat center, child placement services, a radio ministry, and now a publishing resource.

Introduction

Straight Talk with Robert Day offers concise, engaging and insightful principles on issues of leadership, family, culture and ministry. This is a must read for every caring American!

Robert Day is a leading voice in the catalyst of change for children and families in America. Four fundamental convictions drive his passion to restore families. 1. Every sociological crisis facing our culture today can be traced back to the lack of a stable two-parent family. 2. The power to fix this crisis is not with government, but with caring Americans throughout our country. 3. Every child deserves to be loved and motivated. 4. Urgency, in the name of children, is not a vice, it's a virtue.

In addition to a professional career of successful child welfare intervention, Robert speaks from personal experience. Having grown up in abject poverty and experiencing every kind of abuse as a child, Robert knows first hand the urgency facing America's children. Robert chronicles his painful childhood in his biography *Worst of Mothers... Best of Moms.*

In 2011, *Straight Talk with Robert Day* was created as an outreach of Patrick Henry Family Services. The *Straight Talk with Robert Day* radio ministry began with one-minute Straight Talk segments for a country radio station in Brookneal, Virginia. Shortly thereafter, *Straight Talk's* daily one-minute segments landed where they remain today, on Spirit FM, the largest Christian radio station in Virginia. In 2013 a 30-minute *Straight Talk with Robert Day* radio show was launched on WLNI, Lynchburg's News & Information station. The longer, weekly shows gained a good following, and today these segments can be found on podcast at *straighttalkwithrobertday.org.*

Through the radio programs and social media outreach, *Straight Talk* has proven a valuable ministry, and has provided more visibility for the important work of all the ministries of Patrick Henry Family services. *Straight Talk* has also helped propel Robert Day into a sought after speaker for churches, civic groups, conferences and special events.

Many people are wise, but few discern with such clarity and passion as Robert Day; that is what sets him apart as a quality leader, husband, father and friend. I have been blessed to know Robert Day personally and professionally for many years. His genuine compassion for others and his authentic testimony are truly inspirational. Those around him are challenged to live more selfless, intentional, and purposeful lives. I know you'll be challenged and changed as well through **Straight Talk with Robert Day**.

Adam Spencer, Director of Philanthropy, Patrick Henry Family Services

Note to Reader

THE FOLLOWING SEGMENTS were written and recorded for a radio audience. The one minute segments, (actually fifty seconds with intro and outro) were originally intended for audio use. For this book they have been slightly edited for a reading audience. The content itself has not been altered.

The segments have been grouped together into the four sections: Family, Culture, Leadership, and Ministry. These are the areas of life I'm most concerned about, and believe have the greatest opportunities for changing the present reality.

There is a secret pattern embedded in every segment. Let's see if you can find it.

Robert J. Day, CEO, Patrick Henry Family Services

Section One

Family

1 Live Better

ONE OF THE DRIVING FORCES in American culture is the yearning of parents to give their children a better life, with more opportunities than they themselves had. That motivation comes from two healthy sources. Every loving parent wants good for their kids. That's natural. By striving to meet that goal, they are also investing in the future well-being of society. They are paying it forward, so to speak. That too, is natural and good.

I fear though we may have now gone too far. Bolstered by the godly desire to give our children a better life, we've showered them with unwarranted praise, smothered them with unneeded attention, and have given them too much stuff. We have confused giving them what they want, with providing them with what they need.

Indeed, we've given this generation of children a better life, probably the best life of any generation in American history, but what is that if we fail to show them how to live better? That's the real goal.

TAKE AWAY:
Living better is better than a better life.

2 **A Seedling**

THERE'S A TREE IN MY YARD that bends. As it grows, it will eventually break under its own weight. It's inevitable, and that's a shame. I like the tree. It's in a good spot and provides needed shade. When it comes down, it will take years to replace, probably more years than I have left to live.

There's an old Chinese proverb which speaks to the need of every parent to teach their children early: "The best time to plant a tree is twenty years ago." That reminds me of the biblical proverb, "Teach a child in the way they should go when they are young, when they are old they will not depart from it."

The best time to plant wisdom in the heart of my children was twenty years ago. They're adults now, and the direction of their life is pretty much set. It's a great deal more difficult to straighten them out now. They will either stand tall, or fall under their own weight.

TAKE AWAY:
A seedling will grow in whatever direction you set it.

3 **Real Experts**

PARENTS TAKE COURAGE! You are the expert when it comes to your own child. No one can do it better than you. They are your children. They were entrusted to you by God. You know them better, and love them more, than anyone else on the face of the earth.

This doesn't mean you are a perfect parent, or that you'll never make any mistakes. You most certainly will. It does mean that more than anyone else, you care about the well-being and success of your children, and therefore are the best qualified to make decisions on their behalf. Never let anyone ever convince you otherwise.

There is nothing wrong with learning from others. We can all use help in the parenting department. However, in order to be an empowered, confident parent, you must learn to recognize when others overstep their bounds and when it may be appropriate—and even better—to trust your instincts and judgment. You are the real expert when it comes to your own children.

TAKE AWAY:
Parents are the real experts when it comes to their own children.

19

Best Nonprofit

I'M THE CEO OF Patrick Henry Family Services, a ministry that has cared for children for more than 55 years. I've spent most of my professional life working in agencies that serve children in some capacity or another. I'm here today to tell you about the very best nonprofit organization that serves children. No, it's not us. It's the family.

The family is the best qualified institution when it comes to meeting the various needs of children. When in a healthy state, nothing can compete with the family. The family unit is the most motivated, and most efficiently run nonprofit organization that has ever existed.

There are a lot of groups, profit and nonprofit, who exhaust a great deal of resources trying to do what the family was created to do. For every dollar we spend on supporting and undergirding that institution, we will save hundreds of dollars later. There simply is no better investment by society, and for society, than to make sure families are strong.

TAKE AWAY:
The family is the most motivated and most efficiently run nonprofit that has ever existed.

5 **Fair**

THAT IS NOT FAIR! How many times have you heard that in your lifetime? How many times have you said it? I know I've said it—a lot. I have thought it even more. Of course, we grownups understand that it isn't fair, whatever "it" is, because life isn't fair.

One of the rites of passage is learning life is not fair, and there's little we can do about that. Right? Well, life may not be fair, but there is something we can do about it. No, I'm not suggesting we somehow make it fair, because most of the time we can't. Much of life is out of our control, and trying to make everything fair just makes everything worse.

Life is not fair, and there's not much we can do about it. But, we can be consistent. We can be honest. We can be compassionate and kind. And above all else, we can be just. Those things are within our power. Those things we do control.

TAKE AWAY:
Life isn't fair, but we can be.

Character Flaw

THE LORD RECENTLY REVEALED a flaw in my character. He showed me that I am not always appreciative enough, especially of the people in my life. Do any of you have that problem? There can be a hundred reasons why we are lackadaisical about our appreciation but the results are the same — a sad end to a wonderful relationship.

And, you know what they say about that? We don't truly appreciate someone until they are gone. But we don't have to lose someone before we finally learn to appreciate them. I believe there are two perspectives that can help us be more appreciative of others.

First, we must understand they not only want, but also need to be appreciated. When we don't properly express our gratitude it's like we are robbing them of a fundamental need like food or water. And secondly, the most amazing thing about expressing appreciation is what it does for us as well. The more we give, the more we receive in return.

TAKE AWAY:
We need to appreciate the value of appreciation.

7 True Strength

VULNERABILITY IS HARD. Being vulnerable is scary. Few of us are willing to truly expose our thoughts and feelings to others. However, according to Dr. Brene' Brown, who has done extensive research on the subject, being vulnerable is exactly what we need to do to be healthy. She says, "Vulnerability is the core, the heart, the center of meaningful human experience."

You see friends, we can't experience life without feeling life, and we can't feel life without being vulnerable. Vulnerability—the art of being uncalculating, the willingness to look foolish—is the staple of creativity, and the substance of authentic leadership.

Vulnerability is also the very essence of romance; it's the glue that holds healthy relationships together. Without vulnerability there is no genuine community. To truly be happy we must accept the truth that vulnerability is not weakness, it is strength. To be our authentic self may be the most bold and courageous thing we do. I promise you it will also be the most rewarding.

TAKE AWAY:
It's brave to be real.

Third Layer

DESPITE THE FACT CHILDREN enter this world weak and helpless, the Creator designed it so they would be raised by two loving parents: one of each gender so the child would learn from, and relate to, both. With little effort, these two adults are emotionally bonded to their child and will unselfishly, and even sacrificially, protect and serve her every need. But, what if it doesn't happen?

The natural order provides additional support by an extended family. All kinds of resources are there for the young parents. Grandparents, aunts, uncles, cousins, and even siblings, can serve as a second layer of protection and care. But, what if that doesn't happen?

God would then have the Church fill the need. It not only contributes religious instruction and moral support to the family, but also steps in during times of real need with extra resources and assistance. The Church serves as an important third layer of care around those children who are lacking full support from the first two.

TAKE AWAY:
Church is another form of family.

9 The Future

WHEN I WAS TEACHING COLLEGE courses I came to recognize a basic life principle: what people think about their future is much more important to understanding their behavior than what they think about their past.

I realized my students' academic success had little to do with "where they came from" but was determined by "where they were going." Bright kids from good families and strong schools often failed, while average kids from broken families and poor schools often did very well. The difference was what the individual student wanted from the future.

I witnessed so many privileged students waste their time (and their parent's money), not because they had such a horrible past they couldn't overcome, but because they had no concept of their future, or what they wanted from it. Many wandered without purpose through their college years and beyond—failures of prosperity. I also witnessed many students, from challenging backgrounds and limited resources, excel because they knew what they wanted and where they were going.

TAKE AWAY:
Knowing where you are going is the key to success, not where you have been.

10 Sacred Privilege

OTHER THAN DECIDING to make a spiritual conversion and follow Christ with all our heart, soul, mind and strength, the single most important decision any human being will ever make in their lifetime is who they will marry.

Think about it. Choosing the wrong spouse could have all kinds of long-term negative consequences. It could lead to an onslaught of pain and loss including, but not limited to, children being harmed, financial bankruptcy, emotional crisis, physical trauma, spiritual deformity, broken relationships, misguided careers, lost passions, and even stolen identities — a stolen identity of who you were intended to be in Christ.

Unfortunately, our society has become far too careless about this critical decision. Without a devout commitment to seeking the kind of love God created us for, we run the risk of settling for a cheap counterfeit and never experiencing the fullness of love. We must get back to the place in our culture where we treat matrimony as the most sacred privilege this side of heaven.

TAKE AWAY:
Get the marriage thing wrong, and little in life will go right.

11 Pure Religion

IT'S SAD SO MANY CHILDREN have to use all kinds of qualifying adjectives to identify the men who serve as father figures. There are the official ones: step, foster, adoptive, and real fathers (sometimes called biological or birth fathers). At Patrick Henry we have "house-fathers" who professionally care for the children in our homes.

For many kids, even those don't work. They have to get creative, "He is like my real father." Or, they might introduce him with, "He's been like a father to me."

Please don't get me wrong. I'm thankful for all those types of fathers. I praise the Lord for men who stand in the gap and become fathers to the fatherless, to be a dad to those who need one. While not ideal, it's a hundred times better than the child having no father figure at all. I'm convinced that to be a substitute father, officially or not, is the greatest acts of human kindness. The Bible calls it "pure and undefiled religion."

TAKE AWAY:
You don't have to be a real dad to be a good father.

12 **Wrong Reasons**

PEOPLE WHO AREN'T WHOLE, or who are hurting emotionally, often seek after romantic relationships in order to fill a big void in their heart. They have a deep need to be loved, and feel loved.

Of course, it's never the answer, especially for the other person being used as a type of psychotropic medication. The reason is rather obvious. Hurting people tend to hurt other people, especially the ones closest to them. Relationships built on this type of faulty foundation will usually end badly. When they do, it only adds to their pain and sense of desperation. The rebound relationship will be twice as bad

I think it's why my mother had so many failed relationships in her life. Not only was she looking for love in all the wrong places, she was looking for love for all the wrong reasons. She never found it either. Without the security of God's love there'll always be something missing that the romantic relationship will never be able to give.

TAKE AWAY:
There is Love. Then there is love.

13 **Growing Down**

My wife and I raised four children. When they were small they couldn't wait to grow up to do "big kid" things. When they grew up to be teenagers, they couldn't wait to do adult stuff. Yet, when it was actually time to become an adult, they all went into it kicking and screaming. As you can imagine, it wasn't the privileges, but the responsibilities of being an adult, they baulked at.

Growing up is painful. Being an adult is not only hard, it often hurts as well. But, I want us to take this moment to ponder the alternative. What if we didn't grow up, or worse, what if we started growing down—regressing back toward childhood?

I think we probably all know individuals who have. Consider where they are in their lives, and I'm sure you'll agree that growing up is better than growing down. Maturity is the goal of every living thing. It is God's wise design and loving plan for each of us.

TAKE AWAY:
Maturity is the goal of every living thing.

14 Fine Kids

I'VE BEEN WORKING with children and families for a long time. My time at Patrick Henry Family Services only confirms what I have observed in other places; the kids are fine, it's the parents who have issues. Let me explain. We've all been drilled on the concept of the "strong willed child." But, I'm with Mike Mason, what we really have is a problem with "strong willed parents."

We have to believe Jesus when He said that He was telling us the truth, and the truth is that we adults must change and become like our children, or we'll never enter the Kingdom of Heaven. In other words, Jesus said the kids are just fine, it's us big people who have problems.

Perhaps a more grace filled approach to parenting is about letting kids be more like kids. Maybe it's about parents joining their children in play and make-believe. I have little doubt that grace filled parenting is learning from our children everything they can teach us.

TAKE AWAY:
Anyone who does not become like a child, will not enter into the Kingdom of Heaven.

15 **Spinning Wheel**

EVER FEEL LIKE YOU'RE A HAMSTER caught in a spinning wheel? The faster you run, the faster the wheel spins. The faster the wheel spins, the faster you have to run. I think we all do sometimes. We go to work so we can get paid. We get paid so we can eat. We eat so we can go to work tomorrow.

These two verses should be read and meditated on each and every day of our lives. "Seek first his kingdom and his righteousness, and all these things will be given to you as well. Do not worry about tomorrow, for tomorrow will worry about itself. Each day has enough trouble of its own."

I love how this biblical truth is captured by two of my favorite characters in children's literature, Winnie the Pooh and Piglet. Pooh asks Piglet, "What day is it?" "It's today," squeaked Piglet. "My favorite day," said Pooh. We should enjoy today, after all, it is the day the Lord has made.

TAKE AWAY:
Every day should be our favorite.

16 **Grief Agreement**

AUTHOR AND THEOLOGIAN C.S. Lewis married his wife Joy after she found out she had terminal cancer. It was then he knew he loved her. Lewis married her while she lay in her hospital bed, what they both thought would be her death bed.

However, she experienced a remarkable remission and they had some time together as a couple. Eventually though, the cancer won and she died at age 45. Lewis said that the three years of his marriage to Joy were the happiest of his life. The grief he felt after her passing was so deep because of the happiness he had experienced together with her.

According to Lewis, and I think he is absolutely right, "marriage is an agreement to grieve." Marriage is a choice to mourn, because one day we'll all pass away. It may be tomorrow, or it may be fifty years from now. We don't know when, and that's the point. So, live in the marriage like you might die tomorrow.

TAKE AWAY:
It is better to have loved and lost, than never to have loved at all.

17 The Vow

I LOVE MY WIFE. When I say "my wife" it's not the same as saying "my car" or "my house." It's not even the same as saying "my life." She's not my possession. My wife is not some object I may love one minute and curse the next. My love for her is not some fleeting feeling. She's my wife because I'm her husband. The symbiotic relationship is not equal to any kind of object or person on earth.

The kind of love my wife and I share is fully realized in the words of the wedding vow: "To love and to cherish, in sickness or in health and forsaking all others, to cleave to one another for as long as we both shall live."

This vow speaks of a dedication to one another that's found only in marriage. It's a commitment to love always. We will love each other when we are at our best. We will love each other when we are at our worst.

TAKE AWAY:
It is the vow, and the commitment to keep it, that makes marriage sacred.

18 **Being There**

THERE ARE FEW THINGS BETTER than a warm fire on a cold, rainy day. There is absolutely nothing better than family on those cold, harsh, bitter days of life. Family can't always keep those difficult days from happening. As much as they may want, families cannot always stop the harsh elements of this world from invading the sanctuary of their home. However, families can provide warmth and comfort through it all.

Dear parents, you don't have to have knowledge of child psychology to be good parents. You don't even have to be experts at parenting. You just have to be there, to be present when your presence is needed most: to hold their hands, to give them hugs, to kiss their wounds. And, be there to wipe away their tears.

You also have to be there when they are bullied, when their heart is broken for the first time, when they mess up, make a mistake, and fail so miserably. Just be there. That is good parenting.

TAKE AWAY:

To be present when your presence is needed is good parenting.

19 **Discerning Parents**

HERE IS A LIFE LESSON that should be taught at an early age, and recited throughout the rest of our lives: Not every problem is bad and not every opportunity is good.

We do our children a great disservice when we shield them from every problem. It is in struggling, in doing the hard things. that we all grow. There is no growth without struggle. Providing our children an easy path is not the best way to help them. Letting them work through difficulties prepares them for the real life challenges they will face as adults.

Our children must also learn that not every opportunity is good. They must learn to make choices, to see that they can't have it all, and they can't do it all. They must learn to say no to some good opportunities. Discerning which opportunities to take and which to pass is one of the best skills our children can learn from us. Yet, they will need our help to learn it.

TAKE AWAY:
Raising dependent child is a disaster in the making.

20 The Myth

FOR A LONG TIME, too long really, I bought into the common myth that it is the quality of time I spend with my kids, not the quantity of time, that really mattered. I know much better now. Unfortunately, I learned it by experience.

Here is the simple truth of the matter. Quality time only comes from quantity of time. Children and life are unpredictable. No amount of planning, or good intentions, can make quality time happen with our kids. Most of those so-called quality times are unplanned and unexpected, and will happen if we're present or not.

Try as we might, a child's first step occurs when the child is ready not when we are. If we are not there we will miss it. We must find the time to be home. Let's make time to be with our kids as much as possible. The more we are present and plugged in, the more quality time we will have with our children. That is no myth.

TAKE AWAY:
When it comes to our children, good intentions are not good enough.

21 **Losing Battle**

AFTER YEARS OF DECLINE, the number of children living in foster care started rising in 2013. According to federal statistics, about 415,000 children were living in foster care last year. 15% of them hadn't yet passed their second birthday.

Children come into the foster care system for all kinds of reasons. It may surprise you to know that it's neglect, and not abuse, which is the major reason. It may further surprise you to learn that addiction to drugs is the leading cause of those neglect cases.

About 25% percent of child welfare cases in 2013 involved heroin or cocaine. That is up 19% from 2010. A shocking 70% of children in the system less than a year old had parents who were using those drugs. The real challenge is getting the parents to kick the habit, especially when the drug is heroin. It can be a lifelong battle. We are losing the war on drugs, and it is the children who are suffering our defeat.

TAKE AWAY:
When children suffer, we all lose.

22 Dishonorable Behavior

WHY IS IT THAT THE ONES we are the most familiar with, the ones we love the most, are the ones we too often ignore? We don't hear what they are saying—not really. We don't see what they need—not really. We don't stop to consider what they want—not really. Don't you find it odd that we snub the ones we love the most? Why is that? What is wrong with us?

Sometimes we blame our disregarding behavior on being too busy. Other times we blame it on being distracted, or maybe we're just too tired. And, there may be an element of truth to our excuses. We don't mean to ignore them. Well, at least that is what we say to them.

We rarely blame our dishonorable behavior on the true culprit, which is our own selfishness. I am the first to admit I have this problem. So today, I commit to truly be present with all those I love. You?

TAKE AWAY:
We always hurt the ones we love.

23 Narcissism

RECENTLY THE FIRST STUDY on the origins of intense feelings of superiority (or what is known at narcissism) in children was released. Surprisingly, the researchers found that children of excessively praising parents were more likely to score high on narcissistic qualities but not self-esteem. In other words, parents missed what they were aiming for and hit something that is actually a harmful mental disorder.

They concluded that positive feedback to children should be tied to real behavior, rather than piled on indiscriminately, or exaggerations of the facts. Other studies are showing that narcissism is on the rise in young adults and it stems, in large part, to our cultural tendency to focus on boosting high self-esteem. It may be well intentioned, but falsely praising children, and rewarding them for nothing, is backfiring.

Instead of pursuing self-esteem—like it is the pot of gold at the end of the rainbow—we should encourage parents to do things that enforce self-respect in their children. That is better than gold.

TAKE AWAY:
Self-respect is better than self-esteem.

24 Father's Day

THE THIRD NIGHT after the birth of our first child, I was overwhelmed with my new role as a father. My son was crying, my wife was exhausted, and my 24-year-old inexperienced self, was trying to get him to sleep.

As I rocked him, physically weary and emotionally drained, I suddenly panicked at the realization of being responsible for this child for the next two decades. I grew up with many men in my life from my mother's numerous relationships, but I never had a father. Now, there I was with this precious, helpless infant and I had no idea how I was going to be his father.

I did the only thing I knew to do. I drew on the only assistance available. I prayed to my Heavenly Father. Crying as much as my baby boy, I asked the Lord for help getting him to sleep, and for the wisdom and courage to raise him. My Father faithfully answered both of my desperate requests.

TAKE AWAY:
Not having a father doesn't mean you can't be a good dad.

25 **Eating Sugar**

THE STORY GOES that a father and mother brought their son to Mahatma Gandhi and asked him to tell their son to stop eating sugar. The leader of India's non-violent revolution to remove the British from his home land told the parents to come back in three days.

Three days later the parents returned very excited to have their instructions to their son reinforced by such a great and important person. Gandhi looked the young boy in the eyes and said, "Stop eating sugar." Curious that they had to wait, the parents inquired, "Why didn't you tell him three days ago. Why did you make us come back?" Gandhi replied, "I had to stop eating sugar first before I could tell him to quit."

Whether it's true or not, the story teaches a valuable lesson. Parents, don't give instructions you can't obey. Teachers, don't give lessons you don't know yourself. Preachers, don't sermonize what you do not live. Politicians, don't pass laws you refuse to live under.

TAKE AWAY:
Don't preach it, if you aren't living it.

41

Section Two

Culture

1 **Limited Edition**

"LIMITED EDITION." "While supplies last." "For a limited time only." We often see these tag lines on retail merchant goods, or marketing schemes, as a way to make them more desirable and sell faster. I wish young ladies today saw their hearts in the same way.

Girls, listen up. Your love is not cheap. It is not a dollar-store trinket. It is not a rollback priced item at Walmart. Your affection is not to be discounted until it finds a buyer. You are a rare, limited edition. You are a special edition. You're a unique treasure in all of God's creation. Save your heart, and your body, for that special someone God has made especially for you.

Please remember ladies, your irreplaceable value is what should entice a lover, not how easily assessable you are. Without that God given value, you become a cut-rate, generic, transaction to anyone looking for a good deal, rather than the treasured possession of your soul-mate's heart. How rare is your love?

TAKE AWAY:
True love is never cheap.

45

2 Devil's Workshop

ACCORDING TO THE LATEST comprehensive survey of the U.S. juvenile justice system, the number of teens in the system continues a long decline which peaked in the mid 1990's. In fact, there are fewer children in the system today than there were 20 years ago. That's the good news.

The bad news is no one seems to really know why. Some experts think the numbers are simply returning back to a more normal rate after an unexplained high. Others believe the states are doing a better job of diverting the young offenders to alternative programs. No one really knows for sure.

I think the cause could be attributed to something entirely different. I believe it may have to do with the rise of social media and video games. With the surge of electronic entertainment, youth are simply not out in public as they used to be. Idleness is the devil's workshop. I'm just not sure that the new found source of activity is really any better.

TAKE AWAY:
We may have fewer juvenile delinquents because they've become electronic zombies.

3 **Good Intentions**

LET ME ENCOURAGE YOU today to find the good intentions in others. Most people, even those we disagree with, have good intentions. Believe that because it's true. We must learn to give people the benefit of the doubt.

It doesn't mean that people with good intentions don't have bad ideas. They often do. And, it doesn't mean that people with good intentions don't do stupid, and even bad things. They most certainly do. Giving people the benefit of the doubt means we start with the assumption that very few people wish to do us harm, that very few people purposely want to do evil.

We should always start a conversation or a relationship with the element of trust until shown otherwise. I know it's risky, but I also know that it is rewarding. When you start with trust you are usually reciprocated with trust. There are some exceptions to be sure. Nevertheless, we shouldn't allow the actions of a few to determine how we see the majority.

TAKE AWAY:
There's no other way to be successful in relationships than to trust and verify.

4 **Job Love**

LIKE MANY PEOPLE, I have found myself unemployed on occasion. The last time was due to the Great Recession. Millions of us lost our job back then.

I loved my job. I loved what I was doing, and I loved the organization I was doing it for. It was a wonderful job. So, you can imagine my great disappointment when I was told I would be one of many being laid off. Disappointment quickly turned to depression as I tried to make sense of what happened.

A wise person told me something then I wish I had known earlier in my career. He said, *"You can love your job, but your job can never love you back."* Isn't that true. Our jobs can provide income. They can give us a sense of purpose and accomplishment. Our jobs can even be opportunities for personal growth. However, our jobs can never love us. Let us be sure then, we don't lose sight of those who do love us back.

TAKE AWAY:
The purpose of a job is to care for your family, not to be a substitute for it.

5 **You Is**

A SPECIAL WORD to young people today: be yourself. President John F. Kennedy once said, "Conformity is the jailer of freedom and the enemy of growth." That is so true. Mindless conformity is a prison. Have you ever noticed that everyone who is trying to be different looks alike?

You need to find your best self and be it. You can not be anyone else, and no one else can be you. I encourage you to express yourself authentically, and don't be afraid to stand out. At the same time keep in mind you don't need to behave or dress in extreme ways just to be different. You don't need purple hair, tattoos, or body piercings, for example, to be different or special. In the end, it's more important to be respected than noticed.

A wise old country preacher summed up the issue so well when he said, "You've got to be who you is. Cause, if you is who you ain't, you ain't who you is."

TAKE AWAY:
No one can be you better than you.

 Defiance

DEAR PASTORS and denominational leaders. Years of declining membership, shrinking missional giving, political infighting, and growing irrelevance in society, is ample evidence of a major crisis. Denial of the crisis, and responding defensively to questions about the crisis, will not help the situation or accomplish God's mission.

Let's face it honestly. It's not a short term problem, and the long term solutions are going to be hard to come by, but we must be willing to take risks. We need bold leadership. Choosing to maintain is the same as deciding to die. Continuing the programs of the past—only more and better—will not solve the situation: nor will complaining and lamenting. We should be singing doxologies of defiance.

If we're to see the church grow again, and the gospel gain greater share of the culture, we must lead the church out of its captivity. If we desire society to become more like the church, the church must first decide to be less like society.

TAKE AWAY:
The church must be transformed by the renewing of its mind.

7 Life Currencies

WHEN WE THINK OF INVESTMENTS, of investing for returns, we immediately think of money. That's understandable. There are, however, other things more costly than that. Time, energy, and talent are more valuable than gold. They are the real currencies of life. So, the question today is this: in what are you investing those cherished commodities? What is the return on those investments?

No man or woman can afford to devote his or her treasure in anything other than that which lasts, and that which produces greater fold. The Bible says three things remain: faith, hope, and love, and the greatest of these is love. No human being can risk investing their money, time, energy, or talent in any activity or enterprise that does not yield either faith, hope, or love. To invest in any other thing is both a colossal waste of precious resources, and a grave sin against heaven.

Today's a great day to review your portfolio. Are your faith, hope, and love indexes going up?

TAKE AWAY:
Your heart chases after your treasure.

8 Evil Truths

THERE ARE THREE EVIL TRUTHS. First: Evil is real. Evil is more than the lack of good. It's more than being really bad, or really wrong, or really unlucky, or really anything other than really evil. Evil is a category in and of itself, a powerful force unleashed upon all things, everywhere. Nothing, and no one, escapes its reach. But, it's not absolute or eternal.

Second: Don't tempt evil with weakness. Evil is a commanding force, but not as authoritative as goodness and love. Evil prospers in places of physical, mental, moral, and spiritual weakness. There is a saying, "the only thing necessary for evil to triumph is for good people to do nothing."

Third: Evil will show up whatever we do. Evil will test the boundaries of our commitments and the strength of our resolve. Some time or another, the winds of evil will beat against our houses until it finds weakness. We can overcome it through the victorious power of unarmed goodness and unconditional love.

TAKE AWAY QUOTE:
Evil prospers in weak places.

9 Having All

ACTOR AND COMEDIAN JIM CARREY is known for his way-out, bizarre characters. He's become rich and famous by playing the jester. He has reached a level of success few in his industry ever acquire. Sadly, his private life doesn't enjoy the same success.

He once said something I thought was extraordinarily profound for a Hollywood celebrity who is synonymous with foolishness. He said, "Everybody should be rich and famous and do everything they ever dreamed of, so they can see it's not the answer." Wouldn't that be a gift with eternal rewards.

His statement so perfectly falls in line with the theology of the book of Ecclesiastes: vanity, vanity, all is vanity and striving after the wind. Solomon was rich and famous. He tried everything under the sun, and said there were only two things of value—to be happy in your work, and to do good. Everything else, he reported, was temporary and had no lasting value. In other words, having everything is not the answer.

TAKE AWAY:
Having everything is not the answer.

10 Life Business

WHAT'S THE PURPOSE OF LIFE? It's a question as profound as it is common. To put it in a uniquely American vernacular, what is the business of life?

Well, let's first establish what it's not. As much as our society centers on it, the business of life is not business. It's not even about meaningful work, although work is meaningful and essential to a good life. The business of life is not teaching, although education is important. Nor is it serving others, even though I believe service is the secret to joy. The business of life isn't even parenting, without which the world would quickly descend into the chaos of unruly children.

I believe the business of life, the purpose of our existence, is all about becoming a complete human being. The business of life is to pursue the purpose of our creation, and that is to be complete in Him who created us, to be conformed to the image of the one who gave us life.

TAKE AWAY:
Completion in Christ is the purpose of living.

11 **No Argument**

THERE ARE SO MANY PEOPLE working hard every day to make the world a better place. Thank the Lord for that. There are even more people who talk, write, and argue about how to make it better. There's no shortage of debate, and ugly arguments on the subject. In fact, I find it a bit ironic that all the loud discussion and divisive dialogue seems to be making the world a worse place to live. It's hurting, not helping. Thank the devil for that.

I work in a helping profession. It's a great joy, and I'm passionate about what I do. However, at the end of the day, I realize I may not be helping at all. I recognize my efforts may be in vain. It's easy to get discouraged sometimes.

It's at those times I remember what someone once told me; "the only way to better the world is to improve yourself." Yes! That part I can do. That's something I can control, and there's no argument there.

TAKE AWAY:
Improving ourselves is the best way we can make the world better.

12 **Moral Chaos**

IT'S BEEN SUGGESTED by some lately that if you are not angry, or scared, you haven't been paying attention. With so much anger and fear being expressed so loudly, and by so many, we apparently aren't suffering from Attention Deficit Disorder. I would suggest though, we may be lacking proper perspective.

What's the source of all this angst and anxiety? What is troubling us? I think we sense the country is in trouble. We are slipping into moral chaos, and that is a bit frightening. What concerns me most is not blatant immoral acts of individuals, or even forced celebration of ungodly deeds, but rather the impact moral decay has on everything else necessary for a society to thrive.

Moral chaos makes any lawful, worthwhile political progress almost unattainable. People who are preoccupied with public restrooms, or what pronouns to use, no matter how gifted and talented they may be, become prisoners of the unimportant, and their contribution to the greater good is wasted on the trivial.

TAKE AWAY:
Majoring on the minors is a major distraction.

13 **And**

WHICH IS BETTER, being kind or being right? I like to ask people that question. Of course, many try to get out of answering by saying we should do both. I agree. We can be both right and kind, honest and gentle, principled and relational.

However, I like forcing people to give me only one answer. We can't always maximize both of these virtues at the same time, and it's how individuals respond in those moments that reveal a lot about them. It has been my experience most people pick being kind over being right when they are face to face with another human being. But, in a group or a setting less personal, they usually choose to be right rather than kind.

There is a time and a place for everything under the sun. Perhaps there is a time and a place to be right, and another time and place to be kind. Knowing which is which requires a good measure of both truth and grace.

TAKE AWAY:
There is a time and a place to be right, and another time and place to be kind.

57

14 **Hypocrisy**

NO ONE LIKES A HYPOCRITE, even those who are one, and might I add, I am one. Yet, what's the alternative? We probably don't want to live in a world without hypocrites. Let me explain.

Hypocrisy is the practice of claiming to have moral standards or beliefs to which one's own behavior does not conform. That means the only way not be a hypocrite is to not have standards or beliefs. Since no one's perfect, we will never be totally consistent in what we believe, but it doesn't mean we don't believe.

I believe, for example, in absolute truth. When I fall short of that standard and tell a lie, it doesn't mean there's no absolute truth, or that I don't believe in it. The only way not to be a hypocrite is for me not believe in absolute truth. Then when I lie, I'm not displaying hypocrisy. See my point? Matthew Arnold nails the issue when he said that hypocrisy is "vice giving tribute to virtue."

TAKE AWAY:
I'd rather live in a world of hypocrites than in one without standards.

15 **Too Small**

I'M SURE YOU'RE FAMILIAR with the phrase, "too big to fail." It is the belief of political leaders there are some industries so vital to the economic health of our country that they cannot be allowed to go bankrupt. Some banks are too big to fail. The auto makers are too big to fail. I don't know about all that.

I am convinced though, there is something in this country too small to fail, something too tiny to ignore: our children. All children come into this world the same—completely helpless. They are utterly weak and powerless. Their size, age, and immaturity (by that I mean lack of knowledge and experience) naturally make them easy targets for every social ill and human evil.

We cannot fail the children. They need our protection, guidance, focus, and resources. We cannot afford to allow them to be morally bankrupt, intellectually deficient, or emotionally damaged. Their welfare will determine the future of this nation, and that is too big to fail.

TAKE AWAY:
Failing the children hastens the fall of the world.

16 **Chicken Little**

ONE OF THE ADVANTAGES of living for longer than a couple of decades is possessing the perspective that comes from witnessing history, of living through it, and not merely reading about it. I'm a little tickled at today's youth when they get so upset upon learning, or experiencing, something their ancestors would only laugh at today.

The Chicken Little syndrome of believing that the sky is falling, seems to easily disturb the young more than the old. Maybe it's because senior citizens have seen it before. They've lived through it and are still here. Despite the many predictions, the world didn't end.

I think we could use the perspective of the generation that survived the Great Depression, the Second World War, and life before Civil Rights. It doesn't mean we don't strive hard for peace, justice, and equality. It does means though, we don't get so caught up in righting humanities wrongs that we commit graver sins, and by doing so, bring the sky down on ourselves.

TAKE AWAY:
There is nothing to fear more than fear itself.

17 Fatal Depravities

MOST PEOPLE ARE FAMILIAR with the seven deadly sins. A random survey of the populace would show the average person could name at least some of them. In case you need a refresher, the deadly sins that number seven are: pride, greed, lust, envy, gluttony, anger, and sloth. These are the sins of the self, the iniquities of the individual. They are the common evils that so easily plague souls. But, what would the seven deadly sins of society be? What are the perfectly perilous sins of a nation?

Some have said the seven deadly sins of society are these: policies without principles, wealth without work, pleasure without conscience, knowledge without character, commerce and industry without morality, science without humanity, and worship without sacrifice.

Perhaps that's why it feels like our nation is in a death spiral. Yet there's hope. Always. The same power that sets the individual free from the seven deadly sins is the same power that will save our country from its fatal depravities.

TAKE AWAY:
The cure for any sin is the Savior.

18 **Secret Delight**

I'M NOT SURE if I'm seeing a trend that isn't really there, but it seems to me there's a lot of miserable people in the world. The Misery Index is spiking at all new highs. There are many people who are depressed, dejected, discontented, and down in the dumps. In other words, they are miserable. Where is all of this unhappiness coming from? What is its source?

Charles Kingsley explained it best. He said, "If you want to be miserable think of yourself, about what you want, what you like, what respect people ought to pay you, and what people think of you." Yep, that pretty much sums up the problem. As our society has become more self-focused and self-absorbed, we have become more disjointed in our spirits.

We've been told that self-fulfillment is the path to happiness, however the truth is just the opposite. It's when we turn our eyes from ourselves and toward exalting God, and serving others, do we find the secret of delight.

TAKE AWAY:
The promise of self-fulfillment is snake oil for the selfish soul.

19   Worldly Solutions

THERE'S AN INTERESTING STORY in the Gospels of a father whose son is troubled by evil spirits. The desperate man brings his boy to the disciples for help but they couldn't do anything. They didn't have the knowledge or the power. It was only when Jesus appeared that the awful situation was finally resolved.

How many times does the world show up at the church doors looking for help only to find ineffective believers who send them away to seek solutions elsewhere? That is sad. I personally believe that every need in this world can be met by the church. No exceptions. The only reason the church is not addressing vexing issues like child abuse, poverty, and crime, is because the church doesn't believe it can. God's children have been convinced that difficulties of the world are best fixed by worldly solutions.

Nothing could be further from the truth. Only when the church accepts that it possesses both the knowledge and the power, will real solutions appear.

TAKE AWAY:
Every need in the world can be solved by the one institution not of this world.

20 The Branch

HENRY DAVID THOREAU WROTE, "There are a thousand hacking at the branches of evil to one who is striking at the root." There are many who believe that poverty is the root of all social problems. I don't.

I think it's more like the trunk that connects the roots to the branches. As someone who grew up in absolute poverty, and as one who has served the poor in many different capacities, I simply don't believe poverty is the root of all evil.

The root of all kinds of evil, the Bible says, is the "love of money." It is not the lack of money, but rather the love of it. It's true that some people lack money because others love it and have found unjust ways to take it from others. I also believe some people remain poor because a lot of well-meaning do-gooders make their money serving those who don't have it. Their intention are not evil, but the consequences of their self-serving deeds are.

TAKE AWAY:
Good intentions are rarely good enough.

21 **Such Is**

TAKE AN AMERICAN FLAG, spit on it, and set it on fire. What will happen? Many will be indignant at such a thing. Why is that? Think about it. It is only a piece of cloth. It doesn't cost a lot of money. Yet, I think you understand the point I'm making.

The power of the flag is that it is a symbol of something much greater. It represents an idea, a doctrine, a hope for a certain way of life. The people who believe in those things will be angry at such disrespectful treatment of their flag.

How people treat the flag says something about what they think of the country it stands for. I believe the same is true of children. How we treat the most helpless among us, speaks volumes about us. It reveals what we think of their Creator, of the Kingdom He has built for them, of their innocence, and of the loving Father's heart for all. For such is the Kingdom.

TAKE AWAY:
How we treat the most helpless among us speaks volumes about us.

22 **The Tide**

FORGIVE ME if I am exaggerating, but it seems to me we've become a society that would rather worship celebrities than honor heroes. In our media mad mentally, personality now trumps character. I guess that is what happens when a nation of doers becomes a nation of spectators.

We have become a culture that now esteems popularity over truth, where everyone has followers and their worth is measured by the number of likes, hits, and shares they can get, not by their contribution or service to the country. Many have become more motivated by the fear of hurt and rejection than for the search for truth and honor.

Just how do we turn this around? Well, we can decide today we will no longer be a part of the cultural narcissism. We can resolve to swim against the tide. No one has to follow, or like, or share in our counter-cultural protest. Cultures change one person at a time. Let the change we seek start with us.

TAKE AWAY:
Be a doer, and not a hearer only.

23 **Double Dog**

IT HAS BEEN SUGGESTED we make a living by what we get, but we make a life by what we give. It is so true. The blessings of success and prosperity are not found by getting as much as we can, but rather by giving as much as we can.

I know that's counter intuitive. It doesn't seem right. Everyone else around us is frantically scrambling to get all they possibly can. It's like we are all part of a mob at a Black Friday Sale at some major retailer. It seems foolish not to join the fray and fight for our fair share of the limited goodies on the shelves. After all, if we don't, someone else will get that stuff.

But it's all an illusion. I am telling you the truth — getting is not the key to happiness. It never has been, nor never will be. It is in giving that we truly receive. Don't believe me? Try it. I double dog dare you.

TAKE AWAY:
Give.

24   Retail Choices

OUR SOCIETY IS IN TROUBLE. The tidal wave of hedonism washing over this country is destroying the basic foundations of our culture, and it's extinguishing families and doing great harm to children.

We must turn this around. Yet, our hope is not some kind of big, dramatic solution, and we cannot wait for someone else to fix it. There's no grand plan nor noble leader that will save us from ourselves. Cultures change, out of the countless small choices of millions of people. Every citizen matters, and it matters what every citizen does.

We will save this culture one decision at a time. It has to be done retail, not wholesale; person by person, family by family, community by community. More tax money for more government programs is not the solution. Congress cannot pass a law, no matter how comprehensive, that will repair it. While leadership is important, it will not matter what party is in power, or the name of the person occupying the Oval Office.

TAKE AWAY:
It does matter what other people do.

25 Big Rascals

REMEMBER *The Little Rascals* films of the 1930's? Those short comedies were based on the sheer absurdity of children emulating adult behavior: dressing like adults, talking like adults, being interested in adult things. It was funny — then. No one is laughing anymore.

Today, toddlers are wearing suggestive clothing in order to win the Tiara. The language of many eight year olds is filled with adult content and adult language. Twelve-year-olds are not just talking about sex in general, but in specific and graphic detail.

The real dishonor in all of this comes from the so called grown-ups who should know better: parents, for example, who force their children to act adult-like because they're too childish to be like an adult, corporations who pimp adult products and inappropriate entertainment to children in order to make a quick buck, and certain educators who think they can win a future political victory by indoctrinating five year olds with how to think about adult issues. They're the big rascals.

TAKE AWAY:
It would be better to hang a millstone around your neck and throw yourself in the ocean, than to cause one of these little ones to sin.

Section Three

Leadership

1 Focus

HERE'S A LIFE PRINCIPLE to think about today—what you focus on expands. Good or bad, right or wrong, what you focus on will grow. In other words, energy flows to where attention goes. If you focus on the negative, the destructive will grow. If you focus on the positive, the constructive will grow. If you focus on righteous things, virtuous things will expand. If you focus on immoral things, wicked things will expand.

It is simply a fact of life. What you dwell on determines your destiny, because what you focus on sets the boundaries of your existence. You become what you think about, and what you pay attention to.

The questions then to ask yourself today is this, what are you focusing on? What has your attention? Where is your energy being spent? What are the issues or things you are concentrating on? Is there something you want to increase? If so, then make that the emphasis of your thoughts, then watch what happens.

TAKE AWAY:
You reap what you sow.

2 No

PARENTS, TEACHERS, COACHES, employers, leaders of all kinds, this Straight Talk is for you. What you allow, you encourage. That is worth repeating: what you allow, you encourage.

Leadership is about setting limits as much as it is about setting goals. The word "no" is a powerful tool. Perhaps we should use it more often. But, people don't like to hear it, and so we leaders don't like to say it, because it makes us look mean. The truth is, "no" may be the best thing we can say. Sometimes it is the best act of leadership we can execute.

We must appreciate the fact that leadership is not only producing vision but also about providing limits, because leaders must guard the mission and protect the principles that define the group. Leaders, you must enforce the values and rules of your group. It you don't then you are communicating by your inaction that your values are not really your values, and the rules not really the rules.

TAKE AWAY:
No one wins by never saying no.

Mission

I AM OFTEN BEWILDERED by how many nonprofit organizations and churches tend to promote their model or method of service, instead of their mission to service. I recognize that it's easy for organizations to become infatuated with a particular model, and lose the love for their mission. That's not only short-sighted, it's deadly.

To survive the inevitable disruptive forces of change, nonprofits and churches must switch their focus from their trendy models to their timeless mission. Models become obsolete, and the effectiveness of any method decreases over time and under right circumstances, but the mission is always timeless and its scope is beyond any one kind of method.

Nonprofits and churches must focus their attention and resources on their cause, not their systems. They must promote the needs of their clients first, and the needs of the organization second. They should brand the cause for which the organization was started. If they do this, nonprofits can stay relevant and even more so as times and taste change.

TAKE AWAY:
Everything has a shelf life.

4 Seeds

THE ENTIRE UNIVERSE is predicated upon the principle of sowing and reaping. It's a law that can be violated but never broken. Even in business, or the nonprofit world, this code is alive and active. Here are three other ways this law has been expressed.

"What you win them with, is what you win them to." Think about it. It makes sense. If the outreach efforts of a church is focused on programs and entertainment, then they will gain members who don't grow beyond that. The plant is never something different than the seed that was sown.

Here's another one. "You become what you celebrate." Another way to say it, "What gets rewarded gets done." Leaders must grasp that their organizations will rise only to the level of what is honored. What is allowed is encouraged, and what is encouraged is what grows.

But here's my favorite way to express it. "Commitment precedes resources." Plant the seed of commitment, and we will reap the harvest of resources.

TAKE AWAY:
We always reap the fruit of our labor.

5 Enthusiasm

HERE ARE A FEW THOUGHTS concerning the importance of enthusiasm. Norman Vincent Peal said, "There is real magic in enthusiasm. It spells the difference between mediocrity and accomplishment." Similar to that idea is this word from Mary Kay Ash, "A mediocre idea that generates enthusiasm will go further than a great idea that inspires no one."

The secret of success, Winston Churchill believed, "consists of going from failure to failure without the loss of enthusiasm." The secret of genius, Aldous Huxley tells us, "is to carry the spirit of the child into old age, which means never losing your enthusiasm." Vince Lombardi reminds us of the necessity of zeal and passion in the workplace when he famously said, "If you aren't fired with enthusiasm, you will be fired with enthusiasm."

Enthusiasm as defined by Bo Bennett, "is excitement with inspiration, motivation and a pinch of creativity." According to Emerson, "nothing great was ever achieved without it." Simply put, enthusiasm moves the world. So, let's get enthusiastic about enthusiasm.

TAKE AWAY:
Enthusiasm greases the wheels of the world.

6 **Suffering**

HAVE YOU EVER THOUGHT about how much we owe to sorrow and suffering? Perhaps you have never stopped to consider that tribulation has produced some of the greatest written works of mankind. Most of the Psalms, for example, were born in a wilderness experience. Most of the New Testament letters were written in prison.

Even outside of the Bible, suffering has created enduring publications that have become the mainstream of Christian hope and encouragement. The best thoughts of some of our greatest thinkers have passed through the fiery furnace. So many composers of our favorite hymns learned in suffering what they taught us in song. It was in bonds that Bunyan lived the allegory that he afterwards penned. We can thank his chains for that pilgrim's progress.

So, take comfort my afflicted Christian friends. When God is about to make preeminent use of a man or woman, He turns up the heat. He puts pressure on his vessel, and squeezes out of them precious works of art.

TAKE AWAY:
Gold is refined by the fire.

7 **Our Assumptions**

ONE CHRISTMAS MORNING we'd opened all the presents under the tree. Everyone was taking inventory of the gifts they'd received, giving thanks to those who gave them. But my wife, who keeps track of what every child receives, decided that one was missing.

We were both convinced that the package was wrapped in blue paper with a red bow. We searched each child's stack of things. We looked under the tree more than once. We walked through the house looking for the missing present. It wasn't anywhere to be found. Our kids pointed to a package remaining under the tree but we quickly dismissed it as the wrong color.

Finally our oldest insisted, "If it's not that one, then who does it belong to?" We opened it and found it was the lost present, hiding in plain sight. How many times do we search for truth, pray for an answer, and it's staring us in the face, because we've convinced ourselves it doesn't look like our assumptions?

TAKE AWAY:
The only safe assumption is the one you don't make.

Three Kinds

RUSSIAN AUTHOR LEO TOLSTOY believed there were two kinds of people who followed two very different methods of human activity. One uses their reason to learn what is good and what is bad, and they act according to this knowledge. The other act as they want to, and then they use their reason to prove that which they did was good and that which they didn't do was bad.

That certainly is a true analysis, and I would hope to be in the first group instead of the second. However, I believe there is a third kind of person, a rare type, who participates in a special kind of human activity. This group is not opposed to reason, but does use something more profound and reliable to learn what is good and what is bad.

The Christian looks to divine Scripture, and the abiding presence of God's Holy Spirit, to both know and to do what is good, while doing their best to avoid what is bad.

TAKE AWAY:
Faith can be a reasonable approach to decision making.

9 Synergy

TOGETHER WE CAN DO MORE than the total sum of us individually. It's simply the principle of teamwork. There is no substitute for teamwork. When individuals work together a synergy forms that actually creates greater output than all of them do as individuals. It defies math.

We all know that one plus one equals two. Yet, when individuals work together in a synergetic relationship, one plus one can equal more than two. In sports, or in the business world, they call it the big Mo; the big momentum. It's not magic, but sometimes looks like it. Some call it "chemistry," others "the groove," For a church or ministry, it can mean the difference between surviving and thriving.

Acts 4: 32-33, "Now the full number of those who believed were of one heart and soul, and no one said that any of the things that belonged to him was his own, but they had everything in common…. And God's grace was so powerfully at work in them all."

TAKE AWAY:
Two can do the work of three, if they work as a team.

10 **Wet Boards**

WET BOARDS CONDUCT ELECTRICITY, but copper wires do it better. This principle describes the value of effectiveness and efficiency. The mission of a nonprofit or church requires time and energy. There's simply no way around it. Increasing effectiveness and efficiency maximizes the most of those limited assets.

Some are tempted to think that effectiveness and efficiency are conflicting goals, that you can't capitalize both at the same time. However, I believe that is a faulty paradigm that leads to bad decisions.

Nonprofits want to be effective, and they need to be efficient. Doing both ensures the greater likelihood that resources will continue to come their way. Effectiveness means doing the right thing. Efficiency means doing things right. Using a board to conduct electricity, while possible, is not the right thing to do, nor is it doing things right. Get both of those things in proper alignment, and the nonprofits expiration date gets pushed out. The shelf life increases. Death is held off for a little while longer.

TAKE AWAY:
Effectiveness + Efficiency = Power.

11 Complexity Paradox

HERE IS A PRINCIPLE that will take some thought to grasp, but will pay rich dividends to those who get it. The simple is false and the complex is unusable, and by unusable, I mean—unsustainable. Some know it as the Complexity Paradox.

The tendency is to think of problems as simple, but the solutions as complex. By making problems too simple, we may miss finding the real solutions. By making the solution too complex, we may miss the opportunity to solve them.

The more complex the solution, the more opportunity for failure. As automobiles have gotten more complex, for example, there's more opportunity for something to break down or not work properly. And, because they are more complex, it requires the so called expert, and generally a lot more money to repair. For an organization trying to build a program to address a certain problem or meet a certain need, the more complex the program, the greater the possibility something is not going to work right.

TAKE AWAY:
Keep it as simple as possible.

12 Epistemology

EPISTEMOLOGY IS BIG FANCY WORD that means the "study of knowledge." Epistemology tries to answer the question, "how do we know what we know?" There are two ancient ways of knowing something: theology and philosophy, the queen and king of the sciences. Despite their longevity, many today consider them the backwaters of academia.

Academics prefer the relatively new kid on the block in terms of system for knowing something, which is the scientific method. Unlike theology that relays on revelation, sacred texts, and spiritual experience, science is all about observation and measurement. Unlike philosophy that focuses on logic and reason, science is big into tests and repeatable outcomes.

I'm thankful for all three. Each one is valid in its place. I don't fly in airplanes built by theologians, and I don't want my gallbladder removed by a philosopher. At the same time, I don't trust an engineer to build me a bridge to heaven, or a chemist to fix the sin problem that is present in me.

TAKE AWAY:
There is more than one way of knowing something.

13 **Self-Interest**

I AM CONVINCED that every church, civic group, or ministry, no matter its size or resources, is enriched when it fulfills God's mission. But more practically, when churches step out in faith to care for those in need they grow spiritually and God blesses their obedience. They move out of the "Me Box" and become more mindful of others, to live sacrificially, laying down their lives.

All this makes a church more meaningful to a community. It also brings a sense of unity and cooperation as members work together to meet the needs of children and families. I'm not sure who said it, or where I first heard it, but I've remembered it ever since: a healthy self-interest is better than a flabby altruism.

I believe that a church looking out for its own self-interest by investing heavily into ministry for children, is better than a church having a weak and ineffective concern for their wellbeing based on some sense that it's the right thing to do.

TAKE AWAY:
A healthy self-interest is better than a flabby altruism.

14 Negated Message

I FEAR THE CHURCH is shrinking in size and influence, and that means fewer opportunities for children with challenges to get the assistance they need from the community best equipped to help them. I also believe there's a direct link between a dying church and the loss of its special purpose.

The church must be clearer with its message. There's no substitute for unapologetically preaching the Word, confidently proclaiming the Gospel, and zealously participating in evangelistic efforts. None! At the same time I'm equally convinced that the church has a biblically mandated social responsibility that has meeting the needs of children (and by extension, families) at the core. To neglect that mission is to negate the message.

Somewhere along the line, the church abandoned its special call to love the unloved child. Local congregations have largely rejected their unique responsibility of serving the abandoned child, the social orphan, the unwanted kid. In doing so, its religion has become defiled and its power in the world sorely diminished.

TAKE AWAY:
What good is salt if it has lost its flavor?

15 **Keeping Positive**

CONFRONTATION IS INEVITABLE. In fact, there is such a thing as Positive Confrontation. The Bible admonishes, "As much as it depends on you be at peace with all people." That's a worthy goal. But, how do we do it? It may be more practical than you think. Consider these ten ground rules.

1. Focus on issues, not on personalities. That means avoiding personal attacks. 2. Separate your own opinion from the facts as you know them. 3. Acknowledge your hidden agendas. We all have them. 4. Make sure you can restate the views of others before you debate them. 5. Don't interrupt when others are talking. 6. Don't filibuster when it's your turn to talk. 7. Check with all participants, especially the silent ones. 8. No hallway or parking lot discussions. Share in the proper meeting. 9. Wear all your hats during the discussion. Look at it from every perspective. 10. Don't advertise the disagreement, but demonstrate full support of the decision.

Let's keep it positive people!

TAKE AWAY:
Negativity has never produced anything positive.

16 **Others**

IF YOU HAD TO DISTILL the secrets of leadership down to only one word, what do you think that one word would be? What one word unlocks the power of leadership? Is it charisma? Vision? Commitment? Diligence? While all of those are certainly important, I don't think any of them are at the core of leadership. None reveal the leadership secret.

William Booth, a missionary pastor, dedicated his life to helping people in need. One hundred years have passed since his death in 1912, but his remarkable legacy continues today through the many good works of the Salvation Army, which he founded in 1878.

The story goes that on his deathbed, surrounded by family, frail and unable to speak, Booth mustered up just enough strength to scribble one final message on a scrap piece of paper before passing away moments later. The message had only one simple word—"others." Is there a greater legacy? Is there a grander purpose? Is there a better secret to leadership?

TAKE AWAY:
The greatest is the servant of all.

17 Reject Numbness

ONE OF THE GREAT CHALLENGES of our time is not to become numb. There is so much hurt, so much need, and so much conflict in the world today. It is very easy to become indifferent to the pain and problems of others. It is really easy to be overwhelmed by it all.

To save ourselves from emotional overload, we often hide it from our eyes. We deny the harshness of it, or we justify our inaction by reminding ourselves that there is really little we can do about it.

Nonetheless, we can't hide it. We can't deny it. And, we can do something about it. But first we must refuse to be numbed by it all. We must resist indifference. Fight it! Don't be afraid. God will grant you the power to overcome it. The most important things to know and feel in this world are things we need divine strength to comprehend and overcome. Pray for strength. Then open your eyes and get to work.

TAKE AWAY:
The leader must develop a stomach for the journey.

18 Leap

WHEN THINKING ABOUT the quality of good leadership we usually don't think of impulse. Impulse is the instinct to jump before we look. It is the irresistible urge to act. In today's calculating, rational world we want our leaders to have all the answers before making a decision, and we don't want them to make any mistakes. Those who do act on impulse often get it wrong.

However, I think that's exactly why we don't have very many good leaders anymore. It is the fear of acting without all the answers, of making mistakes that keeps good people from becoming leaders. It's the fear of getting it wrong that paralyzes true leadership.

I believe in "blessed impulse"—the ability to blindly move forward because your gut instinct says it's the right direction, it's a good thing to do. Another word for blessed impulse is faith. I think we would all agree that we could certainly use some leaders with a bit more of that these days.

TAKE AWAY:
Without faith it is impossible.

19 **Goodness Sake**

LET'S TALK ABOUT GOODNESS TODAY. Have you ever been tempted by it? Maybe you have never thought about it before. Have you been tempted by goodness? Have you succumbed to the deceitful lure of being good? Please understand that being good can be bad, if being good is only for goodness sake. Goodness can be bad for at least three good reasons.

First—Goodness is bad when goodness evades greatness. Sometimes we are tempted to settle for doing good when we could be doing something really great. Good enough is rarely good enough.

Second—Goodness is bad when goodness avoids service. The world's problems are very messy and unpleasant things. Sometimes our desire for goodness keeps us from diving in and fixing these nasty realities.

Third—Goodness is bad when goodness shuns people. When good people cluster together in their shared goodness, those who aren't so good remain blind to their own needs, but they can clearly see the hypocrisy of those who claim to be good.

TAKE AWAY:
Don't be afraid to get your hands dirty.

20 **Change Agents**

THERE ARE FOUR AGENTS of change, four catalysts that make change happen: Openness, Knowledge, Creativity, and Courage. Anyone of these alone can make change possible. All four working together can guarantee it.

Without Openness, nothing changes. An open mind makes all things possible. Because of Openness, the world is no longer flat. Knowledge is also key to the change process. New information, or a new way of looking at old information, can be the spark that creates change. That makes Knowledge a very powerful tool. Creativity is another essential compound for change. Thinking outside the box has led to many new innovations. From the wheel to the computer, Creativity has led the way. Lastly, Courage is a must. There is no change without it. Change can be scary, but so can the status quo. Therefore, be brave.

Consider this prayer: "God grant us the serenity to accept the things we cannot change, the courage to change the things we can, and the wisdom to know the difference."

TAKE AWAY:
Do you have what it takes to change?

21 The Difference

I WANT TO SHARE a life lesson with you today that could very well change your life. It isn't pleasant. It is usually very challenging to do, and most likely will have a high cost in doing it. However, I promise — better than that, I guarantee — that if you do this one thing on a regular basis it will quickly separate you from the crowd and mark you as a leader.

Here it is: take responsibility for your decisions and your actions. It is as simple as that, and as difficult as that. Take responsibility for your decisions and your actions. Don't play the blame game. Nobody wins playing that silly game. Take responsibility.

I know that it's the opposite of our nature. However, I also know from personal experience that when you learn this life lesson it will make all the difference. The three hardest things to say are: "I did it." "It was a mistake." "I'm sorry." But, saying them has lasting leadership rewards.

TAKE AWAY:
Lead responsibly.

22 **If**

I WANT TO ASK YOU a question that was once asked of me. The question (and my answer) has made all the difference in the world for my life and ministry. Here's the question: If money was not a concern and success was guaranteed, what would you do? In other words, if you had all the money you needed, and you knew for sure that you could not fail, what would you do? What would you attempt: no risks, no fears, no disappointments, only success and accomplishment—guaranteed.

What would you do? The answer to that question, whatever it may be, is what you should be doing with your life right now. Yes, money is a concern, and it's true that failure is a real possibility. However, if there is something you would attempt if those obstacles were removed, then that is how you know what you should be doing with your life right now.

Think about it. For God's children, there is nothing they cannot do.

TAKE AWAY:
All things are possible.

23 **Third Way**

DEAR LEADERS, ARE YOU struggling today with having to make a tough decision? Here is a principle of life that might help you: there is a third way. There is always a third way.

We live in an "either, or" world. We are forced to believe that we either have "this choice" or "that choice" to make. This restricted, narrow way of thinking often forces us to make bad decisions based on limited options. Yet, there is third choice. However, you will not see that third choice, you will not see that third way, until you firmly believe that the world has more "and" than "or."

If you believe there are only two options you simply won't look for any more. But there is more. There's always a third way. It takes creativity and sometimes a great deal of courage, to go against the two established options, but I promise you there is a third way. You just have to look for it. Trust me. It's there.

TAKE AWAY:
Don't think inside or outside the box. Think without the box.

24 **Free Attitude**

WE AMERICANS LOVE our freedoms and rightfully so. The liberties we enjoy are truly rare in world history. However, every freedom we have can be taken away from us. We can lose the freedom of religion. We can lose the freedom of speech, and the freedom to peacefully assemble, for example.

Yet, there is one freedom all people possess. It doesn't matter their age, or where they live, or what kind of government they have. Every tribe and nation around the globe have one special freedom that cannot be taken away by anyone, at any time, or under any circumstance. This freedom does not exist in any constitution or bill of rights.

It is the right to choose your attitude. Psychologist Victor Frankel, who survived the horrors and depravity of a Nazi death camp, wrote in his classic book, *Man's Search for Meaning*, "the last of our human freedoms is to choose our attitude in any given circumstance." Never, ever, let anyone determine your attitude but you.

TAKE AWAY:
When it comes to attitude, everyone is pro-choice.

25   Soul Change

To FULLY UNDERSTAND how to implement real and lasting change, we have to understand the role that culture plays in the change process. Culture is key to change.

If you desire lasting change in a system or organization, you must ultimately deal with the culture of that system or organization. It's true for business and nonprofits. It's true for churches and families. It's especially true for societies and nations. Long lasting change only happens when there's significant cultural adjustment. Why is that?

In a broad sociological sense, culture is a way of thinking for a particular group. It's a way a certain group interprets how the world works, and what it means to be human in that world. It has been said that culture is the "soul of a society." It's the inner spirit of a group or organization. It's in the inward space of the soul that the outward places of the group or organization experience real change. Changing how the group thinks, changes their soul.

TAKE AWAY:
The soul of change is to change the soul.

97

Section Four

Ministry

1 Worry

ARE YOU TROUBLED about something today? A troubled heart is caused by at least two common human temptations: anxiety and discouragement. Anxiety is worry about what might or might not happen. Discouragement is worry about what did or did not happen.

Left unchallenged, these twin troubles of the heart can be costly. They can sap energy, steal away courage, interfere with compassion, and worst of all, they can destroy vision. Sometimes the cure for a troubled heart requires tenderness, and sometimes it demands toughness. Either way, anxiety and discouragement are not to be tolerated by those who believe in the sovereignty of God. These enemies of personal peace must be fought. They must be brought under the submission of faith.

But let not your heart be troubled. The Father has the future covered. There is no place for anxiety. And, the Son has the past covered, so there is no value in discouragement. Believe it wholeheartedly. God is working. Repeat that to yourself as often as necessary.

TAKE AWAY:
Is it a sin to worry? Don't worry about it.

2   Lowly Valley

WHICH DO YOU PREFER? Seeing the mountain from down in the valley? Or, would you rather look at the valley from the top of the mountain? It's a matter of taste. Both are beautiful. Both have an alluring esthetic quality. Best way to see the mountain is from the valley. Best way to appreciate the valley is from the mountain. One serves to glorify the other.

Metaphorically, which do you prefer? Mountain or valley? Here it's not a matter of taste. Spiritually we speak of the mountain being a good place, and the valley bad. Three disciples witnessed the transfiguration of Jesus on the mountain. It was so grand they wanted to stay, but Jesus wouldn't allow it. The need was in the valley, and that's where they would go.

Jesus was compelled to leave the mountain top of Heaven's glory for the lowly valley of human misery. Experiencing the face of God in worship means nothing, if we don't live in the presence of fallen humanity.

TAKE AWAY:
It is in serving people, we truly worship God.

3 Desperation

THOREAU IS OFTEN QUOTED as saying, "Most men live lives of quiet desperation." I don't know about you, but my desperation has not always been so silent. The trauma of childhood abuse, the tenacious impact of poverty, and the pervasive influence of my fallen culture, sometimes caused my inner despair to ooze out in inappropriate and unproductive ways.

Seems to me I'm not alone. There is a growing number of folks whose inner, quiet, desperation is becoming a deafening noise of chaos and dysfunction. Nonetheless, it doesn't have to be that way.

Whether a person's desperation is contained inwardly, or outwardly on full display for all to see, there is a peace which one can possess that surpasses all understanding. It doesn't matter if a person's desperation is quiet or loud, there is a place of rest for any, and all, who seek it. Thoreau didn't know that Christ followers are not most men. We have calmed our quiet desperation by the desperate pursuit of God's presence.

TAKE AWAY:
Desperate pursuit of God quiets our loudest desperations.

4 Grace

RESEARCH IS SHOWING that trauma from abuse, and even from poverty itself, can actually change the way the brain works. We have learned, for example, that distressed children can form new "norms" in their thinking, which then in turn, determines a large part of their behavior.

At Patrick Henry Family Services, we view the children in our care from the perspective of, "what happened to this child?" instead of, "what's wrong with this child?" That does not absolve them of bad conduct. It only provides us a reason behind it. I believe it's a more grace-filled approach to working with children, and adults for that matter, dealing with pattern-controlled behaviors.

Consider the contrast between a ministry based on legalism versus ones based on grace. Legalism demands the individual stop being a perpetrator of sin. Grace pleads with the person to stop being a casualty of sin. Notice how each approach addresses the individual caught in those kinds of negative actions? One gives condemnation. The other offers hope.

TAKE AWAY:
Grace pleads. Legalism demands.

5 Daily Awe

THE DAILY WHIRLWIND of our lives can cause us to mistake the human for the Divine. I may decide to take an alternative route to work and not know the reason why. However, I may unconsciously be obeying a divine suggestion. There are dozens of choices made throughout the day that cause blessings we never know.

Many would call those things merely the result of circumstance, or happenstance. I think that is a fool's explanation. Certainly life is made of chance and coincidence. Yet, it's also made of divine providence and watch care over us. I'd rather believe God's angels are above us, or beside us. I'd rather believe the Holy Spirit provides divine impulse when needed.

Some would call me superstitious, and my way of thinking just hopeful self-deception. I call my perspective a faith driven veneration of the God who holds all things in the palm of His hand. It's a poor life that does not begin the day in awe, and end in worship.

TAKE AWAY:
It's a poor life that does not begin the day in awe and end in worship.

The Byproduct

THE BIBLE SAYS there are things that remain; Faith, Hope, and Love. Of the three, Hope is the hardest to get, and the hardest to give away. Hope is known as the elusive virtue because is so difficult to grasp. It's fairly easy to see Faith in action and Love in operation, but show me Hope. What does it look like?

I find it interesting Hope is listed between the other two spiritual virtues. We can all recognize acts of Faith. We can easily identify deeds of Love. Yet, how does one perform Hope? You don't. Hope cannot be given. It can only be received. Hope is the child of Faith and Love.

If we see someone hungry and say, "I hope you get something to eat," what's that? Nothing. If we act in faith with our possessions, and out of love for the hungry person by providing them food, we have produced Hope. We didn't give it. We gave Faith and Love. Hope was the byproduct.

TAKE AWAY:
Hope is the child of Faith and Love.

7 The World

FOR GOD SO LOVED THE WORLD... He gave. If I were a gambling man, I'd bet you know how that verse ends, and where it's found in the Bible. That famous scripture speaks of something so profound, that despite the fact we've heard it so often, we could be missing the point.

God loved the world. The World? God, loves the world? Yes! He does. He loves the very thing that hates Him. He loves that which hates us. God loves the thing the Bible describes as corrupt, fallen, and evil. In fact, God's love for the world is so strong He gave the only possession He has only one of. Truly amazing!

Why do we, the whosoevers that believed in the precious gift of God, so often stand in judgement of that which God loves? We too often condemn, shun, and disdain that which God loves with so much passion that He sacrificed His only Son. Let all who love God, also love all He loves.

TAKE AWAY:
Let us who love God, also love what He loves.

Wronged

SEEMS TO ME LIKE EVERYONE is trying so desperately these days to make a point. Screaming, protesting, raising a fit to be heard, but they are missing the point. There's something more important than making a point. It's making a difference.

We should never try to make a point at the expense of making a difference. We must remember the mission of Jesus was not to be right, although He was always right. His mission was to be a sacrifice for sin, to love the lost back from their rebellion, to take the hate of the world and nail it to a cross. Being a light to the world is not achieved by winning an argument, but by living a life of meaning and purpose.

Christ didn't leave us here on earth to be right. He left us here to make a difference. He left us here to make disciples. Sometimes the right thing to do is to be wronged, and still love those who wronged us.

TAKE AWAY:
Winning arguments usually doesn't win souls.

9 Divine Blunders

EVER MAKE A MISTAKE? Sure you have. If you are anything like me, you've made plenty. But here's another question, have you ever made a divinely inspired mistake? In other words, have you ever made a mistake that has God's providential fingerprints all over it?

Because the Lord makes all things work to the good for those who love Him and are called according to His purposes, our blunders often look like they were part of God's divine plan, as if He orchestrated our failures for our own good.

Here's what I have learned about that. Those mistakes don't work for our good unless, and until, we acknowledge them as failures on our part. Not only must we own our part, we must also work hard toward not making the same mistake again. Only then will we see anything positive come from the messes we make. When we do wrong, and confess it as such, God begins to make it right. That's amazing, and it's called grace.

TAKE AWAY:
It's never a mistake to trust God with our failures.

10 **Broken Hopes**

EVER SINCE I WAS A YOUNG BOY I've enjoyed spending time in the woods. There's a quiet, peaceful aspect of the forest I find refreshing. It's good for my spirit. If we stop to ponder, we can find many life lessons among the trees.

What makes the trees grow? What gives them the nourishment to survive and even thrive? Look at the base of the woodland trees and you will find the answer. It is dead branches and leaves that the tree itself has shed. The things that have died in the tree is what gives it the power to live. Seems like there's something we can learn from that.

Usually, it's the things in our life that have died, the areas of our life where we have suffered loss, the issues that God has pruned, that give us the greatest potential for growth and new life. Trees are fertilized by their own decay, and so we too are improved by trial and refined by broken hopes.

TAKE AWAY:
Death to self produces abundant life.

11 **Bullies**

IT'S BEEN MY EXPERIENCE that bullies love weakness. They always give into the temptation of it. Evil is like that. It doesn't matter if it originates from powerful spiritual forces, from the darkness of self-centered politics, or from the juvenile mentality of mean kids on playgrounds or computers, if there is weakness it will be exploited.

Even so, sometimes evil just shows up, no matter what we do. Oppressors will oppress. Tyrants will torment. When they do, remember this truth: what happens to us does not say anything about us, but how we respond does.

It's been said that life is 10% of what happens to us and 90% of how we react. The rotten things that happen to us do not diminish our worth. Our identities should never be tied to our victimization. No matter what intimidation we suffer, or the persecution we receive, we are still a precious soul, loved by God, with gifts to give to the world. We should never doubt that. Ever!

TAKE AWAY:
Nothing shall separate us from the love of God.

12 **Universal Constant**

MORE AND MORE I am struck by an increasing awareness of the impermanence of all things. It is a universal truth that I'm learning to embrace. All things have a shelf-life. Everything has an expiration date. Things get old. Things fall apart. Things stop working. Things die, or just become useless. There is absolutely nothing that is not in the process of perishing or changing.

Inanimate things like fashion become dated. Fads die out. Even ideas can become old and moldy. Concepts and models lose their freshness and become stale. Yet, we often carry on as if nothing has changed, resistant to the inevitable march of time. Despite the obvious, we hang onto these things anyway, perhaps because we're emotionally attached, or because we mistakenly believe we can tweak this, or change that, and revive their newness.

Nonetheless, everything has a season. The Bible tells us there is a time and purpose for everything under the sun. Change, dear friend, is the one and only universal constant.

TAKE AWAY:
Change or die. Those are the only two options.

13 **Be Stupid**

SOMETIMES IT'S JUST BEST to be stupid. When dealing with a problem that you cannot solve, the smartest thing you can do is to be dumb.

We all deal with new information by using a mental mechanism called Confirmation Bias. That means people tend to listen, focus on, and remember that which confirms their beliefs, and they tend to ignore and forget what does not. We want new information to confirm what we already think or believe, or else we face the internal conflict of being wrong. None of us want to be wrong. The longer we have held a belief the more we use Confirmation Bias.

However, the greatest discoveries and inventions were made by individuals who were willing to be completely stupid. They turned off their selective thinking long enough to receive new information which allowed them to think differently about a problem or need. It was once believed that man could never fly. The Wright brothers were dumb enough to learn that we can.

TAKE AWAY:
Being smart can sometimes get in our way.

14 The One

THE BEAUTIFUL GOSPEL STORY of the ten lepers being healed is a powerful lesson in gratitude. Ten needy individuals were healed, but only one turned back to give thanks to the great physician who healed him. It should be noted though, that our Lord did not recall His gift from the other nine because of their lack of gratitude. The gifts of God, the Bible says, are irrevocable.

That does not mean we can be unappreciative with what is given or done for us. Not at all! The scripture admonishes us to "always give thanks in all things."

The lesson of the nine ungrateful lepers continuing on with their blessings from God, should teach us to be cautious about our own motivations. When we begin to withhold our acts of kindness and helpfulness, because we think those who receive do not properly appreciate what is done for them, it's time to question our own intentions. We don't serve to be thanked. We serve because we are thankful.

TAKE AWAY:
Check your heart before you give, help, or serve another.

15 Blessed

IN CIVILIZATIONS BASED on a Judeo-Christian ethic, children fare the best; far better than their counterparts in other parts of the world. Why? Long ago these cultures discovered the concept of childhood.

The idea of childhood is not universal. Despite what others claim, childhood was not invented by a capitalist society which could afford to carve out a special, privileged period of time for their offspring. Childhood was discovered in that sacred story of Jesus blessing the little ones. Throughout history, and even today in many parts of the world, children are treated as small adults. They are forced to work, consume, make war, and sin like adults.

In our own country, these destructive attitudes are rising as the church's influence diminishes. I firmly believe the fate of children is connected to the strength of the church. The strength of the church is bound to its conduct toward children. For better or worse, they are permanently fastened. May we bless the children, and be blessed by them.

TAKE AWAY:
Suffer not the little children.

16 Indignant

THE BEAUTIFUL STORY of Jesus blessing the children is found in all three of the synoptic gospels, but Mark's unique account records that Jesus became indignant and rebuked His disciples for preventing the children from coming to Him. Can you imagine Jesus being indignant?

Indignant is a strong word that describes a powerful emotion. Indignation is a special kind of anger. It comes from a belief or feeling that someone is being treated unfairly. The disciples were treating the children unfairly. They were discriminating against them by not allowing them to come to Jesus, and that made Jesus furious. How could these men, who had spent so much time with Him, not know His heart on that issue?

There is no more honorable service, with the greatest potential for impact, with the most amount of good, than to bless a helpless child. C.S. Lewis, that great theologian and author, once said "Children are not a distraction from more important work. They are the most important work."

TAKE AWAY:
Jesus loves the little children, all the children of the world.

17 The Unbelievable

THE VALUE OF CHRISTIANITY lies precisely in that it is not always rational, philosophical, or external. Its usefulness lies in the unforeseen, the miraculous, and the extraordinary.

Christianity, as opposed to the philosophies of man, attracts reckless devotion because it demands absolute faith. The philosopher and the scientist aspire to explain away all mysteries, to dissolve them into the light of human reason. It is natural for the natural man to attempt to put all things in a test tube so they can observed, explain, and control all things. But Christianity on the other hand, demands and passionately pursues the mysterious. In fact, it is the unknown of the supernatural, not the predictability of the natural, which constitutes the very essence of worship.

The first verse of chapter eleven in the book of Hebrews explains it well,.. Christian faith is the "substance of things hoped for, and the convictions of things not seen." In other words, the value of Christian faith is that it believes the unbelievable.

TAKE AWAY:
The value of faith is priceless.

18 **Self-Love**

DO YOU EVER GET DISCOURAGED? Sure, we all do. Discouragement is a temptation that is common to man. But, have you ever thought about where it comes from? Until recently, I thought discouragement was associated with the circumstances that made me discouraged; something didn't happen that I wanted to happen, or vise versa, something happened I didn't want to happen. I thought discouragement was something outside of my control.

Oswald Chambers, the famous author of *My Utmost for His Highest*, described discouragement in a way I have never considered before. He says discouragement is "disillusioned self-love." Ouch, that hurt!

Discouragement happens when our self-centered ego is confronted by reality. Our god complex is shattered by the realization that what we want (even if it is good and noble) is not the will of the universe. So rejoice. Discouragement can be our friend, our tutor to help us be less self-absorbed and more reliant on God. May we stand up to discouragement for the ego trip it is.

TAKE AWAY:
All things work together for the good.

19 **Their Day**

LET ME GIVE YOU A BIT of advice that will make someone's day better, and won't cost you a single thing. Call the waitress, cashier, and other service folks by their name. Look for their name tag, ask if you need to, but call them by name. Smile. Be friendly. Treat them with dignity. They will have a better day, and chances are you'll get better service.

It has been said that you can tell a lot about a person by the way they treat people who have no power over them. What can the waitress or cashier tell about you? Is it consistent with how you act at church or among your friends? Is it in keeping with what you are teaching your children? Is it the way you would want to be treated if you were in their place?

They are people with feelings too. A smile and friendly gesture from you could be a huge blessing to them. So, go ahead, make their day.

TAKE AWAY:
Do unto others, as you would have them do unto you.

20 **Holy Conscience**

WE'RE OFTEN ADMONISHED to follow our own conscience when making a difficult decision. We are asked to let it be our guide when the choice is unclear. Yet, we know that our conscience can be mistaken. It can lead us to do the wrong thing, or to do the right thing for the wrong reason. Following our conscience may lead to a huge blunder. Nevertheless, is it a sin to follow it?

John Foster answers that question this way. "If our conscience be mistaken because we have not taken due trouble to enlighten it, then for that neglect of cultivating our conscience we are responsible."

You see dear friends, our conscience, that inner monitor that all people possess, is fallen and gives off a faulty light. Following it without question is dangerous. However, a conscience fed a daily diet of the Holy Scriptures, guided unceasingly by the Holy Spirit, and singularly serving a holy cause, will never be mistaken. A conscience submitted to God can be followed.

TAKE AWAY:
Trust your gut, only if your gut is sanctified daily.

21 **Resources**

I DON'T KNOW WHO FIRST said it, or where I first read it, but it has radically changed the way I work and live; "Commitment precedes resources." I know it doesn't sound profound, but give it some time. Commitment precedes resources.

Most people hold their commitment to an action or a cause until they see evidence of the resources needed to act. Or, they falsely assume that great deeds are only accomplished by those who first had the resources to accomplish those things. Truth is, the laws of the universe are just the opposite. Assets become available and flow toward those who make great commitments. The created order responds to faith.

Want to feed the hungry, care for the homeless, or maybe share the Good News with the world? Don't wait for the resources. Make the commitment to do those things God has placed in your heart, then look for the things you need. They will begin to appear because commitment always comes before resources — every time.

TAKE AWAY:
Commitment is the currency in the economy of God.

22   **Real Life**

I THINK WE ALL RECOGNIZE that the population, in general, is spending too much time in front of electronic screens just watching. Oh, we might be using our thumbs to manipulate what we are viewing, but it's still passive viewing. All that gawking is turning our children, in particular, into a generation of spectators and voyeurs. They'd rather watch life go by than jump in and get involved.

We must understand that, to some degree, it's natural. It's natural, in that it's fallen human nature. Observing instead of doing has certain rewards: less messy, less risk, and less pressure. Real life is chaotic. It doesn't always end well. Few people live happily ever after. You can't push the reset button.

Real life is risky. There's loss. There's death. Real life is full of pressure and stress. Watching, observing, and cheering on others has none of those ugly realities. But, God designed us to be doers. He made us to be achievers. He saved us to be overcomers.

TAKE AWAY:
Life is meant to be experienced.

23   **Our Post**

MANY SAY THAT we're in Last Times. Seeing darkness abound and evil advancing, what are we Christians to do? Hear the words of Evangelist.

"When Pompeii was destroyed, there were very many buried in the ruins of it, who were afterwards found in very different situations. There were some found who were in the streets, as if they had been attempting to make their escape. There were some found in deep vaults, as if they had gone there for security. There were some found in lofty chambers: but where did they find the Roman sentinel? They found him standing at the city gate, with his hand still grasping the war weapon, where he had been placed by his captain; and there, while the Heaven threatened him; there, while the lava steam rolled, he had stood at his post; and there, after a thousand years had passed away, was he found. So let Christians stand to their duty, in the post at which their Captain has placed them."

TAKE AWAY:
Serve where God has put you until you are relieved of duty.

24 Identity

IDENTITY POLITICS is causing a great deal of controversy and conflict these days. Whether it's gender, race, or culture, there is mounting pressure to side with some identity group and demand our rights. However, there's a higher recognition that could unite us all.

At the very core of every human being is the need to be secure in their identity. The Bible says, before we were born, Christ knew us. We are all His children, called with a specific and special purpose. For anyone today who has the opportunity to have influence in a child or family struggling with issues of identity, it is imperative that we view them as one who bears the fingerprints of God.

They are indeed unique in all of God's creation. They are loved. Male or female, short or tall, black, white, or brown, every person has a reason for being. There's a plan for their life, and the key to knowing that plan is through discovering their distinct identity in Christ.

TAKE AWAY:
We are all precious in His sight.

25 Relevance

THERE ARE MANY REASONS people are avoiding or leaving church today. Yet, there are only four common causes. 1. People feel judged. 2. They don't want to be lectured. 3. Christians are hypocrites. 4. They don't see the God that's being presented in church as relevant to their lives.

All four rationales are interrelated. Relevance is the buzzword. The mantra we consistently hear is that "the church isn't relevant today." But how does the church stay relevant in an ever moving, ever changing, ever demanding society, while upholding God's unchanging Word and timeless principles?

To me, something is relevant if it's what I am seeking. If I go to the store for a hammer and dresses are on sale, that's wasted on me...it's simply not relevant, it's not what I am seeking. But, isn't that the problem? Church isn't about what I'm seeking, it's about what God is seeking. It is God who is seeking me. In the end I'm just seeking my own fallen desires.

TAKE AWAY:
Church isn't about what I'm seeking, it's about what God is seeking.

About the Author
ROBERT J. DAY
MSW, MDV

Married
Father of 4
CEO of Patrick Henry Family
Services
Broadcast Host of Straight Talk
Author

Born to an unwed, teenaged mother, Robert's childhood of poverty and abuse included more than 35 temporary homes before his unlikely graduation from high school. Today, through God's grace, and with two Masters degrees in hand, Robert's life work is dedicated to keeping children safe and families strong. As CEO of Patrick Henry Family Services, Robert is successfully leading the organization to the forefront in the child welfare industry. His vision and leadership for a revolution in residential care and counseling have proven effective. Robert has also built a strong following as the host of Straight Talk, a popular, daily broadcast. His moving, inspiring testimony, together with his unique and timely perspective, has made Robert Day a sought after speaker for conferences, churches, civic audiences and beyond.

robertjdayauthor.org | patrickhenry.org

Patrick Henry Family Services

Patrick Henry Family Services
is a faith-based, 501c3, non-profit
which has been serving the children, families and
communities of
Central Virginia since 1961.

Sustained entirely through donations,
Patrick Henry Boys and Girls Homes,
Hope for Tomorrow counseling,
Safe Families for Children,
Hat Creek Camps,
The Hammersley Center at Hat Creek,
Straight Talk Radio
and many other dynamic programs, all work together to
accomplish the mission of keeping children safe and families
strong.

To learn more, or to discover how you can be involved
with this vital ministry,
call us today at 434.376.2006, or go to
patrickhenry.org.

Book 1 - Worst of Mothers…Best of Moms

Born to an unwed, teenage mother, his
childhood of poverty, neglect and unspeakable
abuse included more than 35 homes before
his unlikely graduation from high school.
Today, as CEO of Patrick Henry Family Services,
Robert Day's life work is dedicated to keeping
children safe and families strong. 'Worst of
Mothers…Best of Moms', is a moving and
inspirational story of hope and restoration,
and provides a new perspective on the
sovereignty of God.

Book 2 - Desperately Healed…My Journey to Wholeness

Surviving the kind of oppressive poverty, neglect and
terrifying abuse Robert Day suffered as a child
implores the question asked by so many; 'how did you
get out…how did you find healing?' Childhood trauma
leaves an intensely painful wound on the adult, long
after the child is grown. In this, his second of a three-
part series, Robert shares the emotions, mistakes and
often excruciating steps necessary to find, and
eventually embrace, that place of 'wholeness'.

Book 3 - Liberty or Death…Leading a Revolution in Child Welfare

Grown, desperately healed and successfully leading a nonprofit ministry in the child welfare industry, author Robert
Day questions why preventable abuse still continues, as it
did in his own story. This third and final book in the
'Rescuing Children…Healing Adults' series provides a
painfully transparent look at how our broken culture and
dysfunctional systems have treated the most helpless
among us. But there is hope; through innovative, Christ-
centered, common-sense approaches, the child welfare
system and the church can remold history and revision the
future to help keep children safe and restore shattered
families…a revolution in child welfare.

Robert Day has dedicated his adult life to child welfare issues. Over those years, many have been moved by excerpts from his incredibly painful childhood. God has now opened the door for this full, gripping account, detailing Robert's struggle through poverty, rejection, hunger and abuse. 'Worst of Mothers...Best of Moms' will move you to tears, but will also inspire...bringing you to your feet as you celebrate the wonder of God's endless grace.

- Tim Clinton, Ed.D., American Association of Christian Counselors President

I have known Robert Day for a number of years and have been thoroughly impressed with his great love for ministry. He has had a profound impact on so many young people who have had the privilege of being blessed by his story. Now, we can all be blessed through his brand new book, "Worst of Mothers...Best of Moms." I encourage you to read it, ponder its message, and allow it to motivate you to serve God through serving others.

- Jonathan Falwell, Pastor, Thomas Road Baptist Church, Lynchburg, VA

In today's world with all the rhetoric concerning the "war on poverty" who better to lead that battle than Robert J Day. We have been friends for over 40 years, we've climbed those Appalachian mountains in eastern Kentucky and managed to walk away "more than conquerors ". Robert's insight and personal life stories prove the Biblical truth "with God, all things are possible". **My prayer** is that this book will move the reader to be "doers of the word and not hearers only". **My challenge** is for us all to honor God and be a blessing to others. It is my joy to call Robert my friend and my brother in Christ.

- Marvin Brown, IT Analyst Senior, Mobile AL

I read Robert Day's first book, Worst of Mothers...Best of Moms. It will tear at your heartstrings! To think a child is subjected to such treatment is unthinkable. Now Robert calls our attention to valuable lesson he learned in his life and work. God continues to have His hands on Robert.
Claudia Cope, Anchorage AK

Worst of Mothers...Best of Moms shows us the power of God to take an unimaginable situation and turn it into something wonderful. It is proof positive that no matter what has happened in our lives, God will deliver us and use us for His glory! Thank you, Robert Day, for sharing your story and showing the world there is hope for all!
Janelle Siler Stephens, Somerset, KY